The Writings of Victorinus

The Writings of Victorinus

The Writings of Victorinus

© Lighthouse Publishing 2025

Written by: Victorinus (Unknown – 304 AD)
Translated by: Rev. Robert Ernest Wallis, Ph.D. (1820-1900)
Updated into Modern U.S English: A.M. Overett (b.1960)

All rights reserved. Without limiting the rights under copyright reserved above, no part of this publication may be reproduced, stored in a retrieval system, or transmitted, in any form or by any means (electronic, mechanical, photocopying, recording or otherwise), without the prior written permission of the copyright owner of this book.

Published by
Lighthouse Publishing
SAN 257-4330
228 Freedom Parkway
Hoschton, GA 30548
United States of America

www.lighthousechristianpublishing.com

The Writings of Victorinus

ON THE CREATION OF THE WORLD

To me, as I meditate and consider in my mind concerning the creation of this world in which we are kept enclosed, even such is the rapidity of that creation; as is contained in the book of Moses, which he wrote about its creation, and which is called Genesis. God produced that entire mass for the adornment of His majesty in six days; on the seventh to which He consecrated it . . . with a blessing. For this reason, therefore, because in the septenary number of days both heavenly and earthly things are ordered, in place of the beginning I will consider of this seventh day after the principle of all matters pertaining to the number of seven; and as far as I shall be able, I will endeavor to portray the day of *the divine* power to that consummation.

In the beginning God made the light, and divided it in the exact measure of twelve hours by day and by night, for this reason, doubtless, that day might bring over the night as an occasion of rest for men's labors; that, again, day might overcome, and thus that labor might be refreshed with this alternate change of rest, and that repose again might be tempered by the exercise of day. "On the fourth day He made two lights in the heaven, the greater and the lesser, that the one might rule over the day, the other over the night,"—*the lights of* the sun and moon and He placed the rest of the stars in heaven, that they might shine upon the earth, and by their positions distinguish the seasons, and years, and months, and days, and hours.

Now is manifested the reason of the truth why the fourth day is called the Tetras, why we fast even to the ninth hour, or even to the evening, or why there should be a passing over even to the next day. Therefore this world of ours is composed of four elements—fire, water, heaven, earth. These four elements, therefore, form the quaternion of times or seasons. The sun, also, and the moon constitute throughout the space of the year four seasons—of spring, summer, autumn, winter; and these seasons make a quaternion. And to proceed further still from that principle, lo, there are four living creatures before God's throne, four Gospels, four rivers flowing in paradise; four generations of people from Adam to Noah, from Noah to Abraham, from Abraham to Moses, from Moses to Christ the Lord, the Son of God; and four living creatures, *viz.*, a man, a calf, a lion, an eagle; and four rivers, the Pison, the Gihon, the Tigris, and the Euphrates. The man Christ Jesus, the originator of these things whereof we have above spoken, was taken prisoner by wicked hands, by a quaternion *of soldiers*. Therefore on account of His captivity by a quaternion, on account of the majesty of His works,—that the seasons also, wholesome to humanity, joyful for the harvests, tranquil for the tempests, may roll on,—therefore we make *the fourth day* a station or a supernumerary fast.

On the fifth day the land and water brought forth their progenies. On the sixth day the things that were wanting were created; and thus God raised up man from the soil, as lord of all the things which He created upon the earth and the water. Yet He created angels and archangels before He created man, placing spiritual beings before earthly ones. For light was made before sky and the earth. This sixth day is called *parasceve,* that is to say, the preparation of the kingdom. For He perfected Adam, whom *He made* after His image and likeness. But for this reason He completed His works before He created angels and fashioned man, lest perchance they should falsely assert that they had been His helpers. On this day also, on account of the passion of the Lord Jesus Christ, we make either a station to God, or a fast. On the seventh day He rested from all His works, and blessed it, and sanctified it. On the former day we are accustomed to fast rigorously, that on the Lord's Day we may go forth to our bread with giving of thanks. And let the *parasceve* become a rigorous fast, lest we should appear to observe any Sabbath with the Jews, which Christ Himself, the Lord of the Sabbath, says by His prophets that "His soul hateth;" which Sabbath He in His body abolished, although, nevertheless, He had formerly Himself commanded Moses that circumcision should not pass over the eighth day, which day very frequently happens on the Sabbath, as we read written in the Gospel. Moses, foreseeing the hardness of that people, on the Sabbath raised up his hands, therefore, and thus *figuratively* fastened himself to a cross. And in the battle they were sought for by the foreigners on the Sabbath-day, that they might be taken captive, and, as if by the very strictness of the law, might be fashioned to the avoidance of its teaching.

And thus in the sixth Psalm for the eighth day, David asks the Lord that He would not rebuke him in His anger, nor judge him in His fury; for this is indeed the eighth day of future judgment, which will pass beyond the order of the sevenfold arrangement. Jesus also, the son of Nave, the successor of Moses, himself broke the Sabbath-day; for on the Sabbath-day he commanded the children of Israel to go round the walls of the city of Jericho with trumpets, and declare war against the aliens. Matthias also, prince of Judah, broke the Sabbath; for he slew the prefect of Antiochus the king of Syria on the Sabbath, and subdued the foreigners by pursuing them. And in Matthew we read, that it is written Isaiah also and the rest of his colleagues broke the Sabbath—that that true and just Sabbath should be observed in the seventh millenary of years. Wherefore to those seven days the Lord attributed to each a thousand years; for thus went the warning: "In Thine eyes, O Lord, a thousand years are as one day." Therefore in the eyes of the Lord each thousand of years is ordained, for I find that the Lord's eyes are seven. Wherefore, as I have narrated, that true Sabbath will be in the seventh millenary of years, when Christ with His elect shall reign. Moreover, the seven heavens agree with those days; for thus we are warned: "By the word of the Lord were the heavens made, and all the powers of them by the spirit of His mouth." There are seven spirits. Their names are the spirits which abode on the Christ of God, as was intimated in Isaiah the prophet: "And there rests upon Him the spirit of wisdom and of understanding, the spirit of counsel and might, the spirit of wisdom and of piety, and the spirit of God's fear hath filled Him." Therefore the highest heaven is the heaven of wisdom; the second, of understanding; the third, of counsel; the fourth, of might; the fifth, of knowledge; the sixth, of piety; the seventh, of God's fear. From this, therefore, the thunders bellow, the lightnings are kindled, the fires are heaped together; fiery darts appear, stars gleam, the anxiety caused by the dreadful comet is aroused. Sometimes it happens that the sun and moon approach one another, and cause those more than frightful appearances, radiating with light in the field of their aspect. But the author of the whole creation is Jesus. His name is the Word; for thus His Father says: "My heart hath emitted a good word." John the evangelist thus says: "In the beginning was the Word, and the Word was with God, and the Word was God. The same was in the beginning with God. All things were made by Him, and without Him was nothing made that was made." Therefore, first, was made the creation; secondly, man, the lord of the human race, as says the apostle. Therefore this Word, when it made light, is called Wisdom; when it made the sky, Understanding; when it made land and sea, Counsel; when it made sun and moon and other bright things, Power; when it calls forth land and sea, Knowledge; when it formed man, Piety; when it blesses and sanctifies man, it has the name of God's fear.

Behold the seven horns of the Lamb, the seven eyes of God—the seven eyes are the seven spirits of the Lamb; seven torches burning before the throne of God seven golden candlesticks, seven young sheep, the seven women in Isaiah, the seven churches in Paul, seven deacons, seven angels, seven trumpets, seven seals to the book, seven periods of seven days with which Pentecost is completed, the seven weeks in Daniel, also the forty-three weeks in Daniel; with Noah, seven of all clean things in the ark; seven revenges of Cain, seven years for a debt to be acquitted, the lamp with seven orifices, seven pillars of wisdom in the house of Solomon.

Now, therefore, you may see that it is being told you of the unerring glory of God in providence; yet, as far as my small capacity shall be able, I will endeavor to set it forth. That He might re-create that Adam by means of the week, and bring aid to His entire creation, was accomplished by the nativity of His Son Jesus Christ our Lord. Who, then, that is taught in the law of God, who that is filled with the Holy Spirit, does not see in his heart, that on the same day on which the dragon seduced Eve, the angel Gabriel brought the glad tidings to the Virgin Mary; that on the same day the Holy Spirit overflowed the Virgin Mary, on which He made light; that on that day He was incarnate in flesh, in which He made the land and water; that on the same day He was put to the breast, on which He made the stars; that on the same day He was circumcised, on which the land and water brought forth their offspring; that on the same day He was incarnated, on which He formed man out of the ground; that on the same day Christ was born, on which He formed man; that on that day He suffered, on which Adam fell; that on the same day He rose again from the dead, on which He created light? He, moreover, consummates His humanity in the number seven: of His nativity, His infancy, His boyhood, His youth, His young-manhood, His mature age, His death. I have also set forth His humanity to the Jews in these manners: since He is hungry, is thirsty; since He gave food and drink; since He walks, and retired; since He slept upon a pillow; since, moreover, He walks upon the stormy seas with His feet, He commands the winds, He cures the sick and restores the lame, He raises the blind by His speech,—see ye that He declares Himself to them to be the Lord.

    The day, as I have above related, is divided into two parts by the number twelve—by the twelve hours of day and night; and by these hours too, months, and years, and seasons, and ages are computed. Therefore, doubtless, there are appointed also twelve angels of the day and twelve angels of the night, in accordance, to wit, with the number of hours. For these are the twenty-four witnesses of the days and nights which sit before the throne of God, having golden crowns on their heads, whom the Apocalypse of John the apostle and evangelist calls elders, for the reason that they are older both than the other angels and than men.

COMMENTARY ON THE APOCALYPSE OF THE BLESSED JOHN

From the first chapter.

1. "The Revelation of Jesus Christ, which God gave to Him, and showed unto His servants things which must shortly come to pass, and signified it. Blessed are they who read and hear the words of this prophecy, and keep the things which are written."] The beginning of the book promises blessing to him that reads and hears and keeps, that he who takes pains about the reading may thence learn *to do* works, and may keep the precepts.

4. "Grace unto you, and peace, from Him which is, and which was, and which is to come."] *He is*, because He endures continually; *He was*, because with the Father He made all things, and has at this time taken a beginning from the Virgin; *He is to come*, because assuredly *He will come* to judgment.

"And from the seven spirits which are before His throne."] We read of a sevenfold spirit in Isaiah,— namely, the spirit of wisdom and of understanding, the spirit of counsel and might, of knowledge and of piety, and the spirit of the fear of the Lord.

5. "And from Jesus Christ, who is the faithful witness, the first-begotten of the dead."] In taking upon

Him manhood, He gave a testimony in the world, wherein also having suffered, He freed us by His blood from sin; and having vanquished hell, He was the first who rose from the dead, and "death shall have no more dominion over Him," but by His own reign the kingdom of the world is destroyed.

6. "And He made us a kingdom and priests unto God and His Father."] That is to say, a Church of all believers; as also the Apostle Peter says: "A holy nation, a royal priesthood."

7. "Behold, He shall come with clouds, and every eye shall see Him."] For He who at first came hidden in the manhood that He had undertaken, shall after a little while come to judgment manifest in majesty and glory. And what says He?

12. "And I turned, and saw seven golden candlesticks; and in the midst of the seven golden candlesticks one like unto the Son of man."] He says that He was like Him after His victory over death, when He had ascended into the heavens, after the union in His body of the power which He received from the Father with the spirit of His glory.

13. "As it were the Son of man walking in the midst of the golden candlesticks."] He says, in the midst of the churches, as it is said in Solomon, "I will walk in the midst of the paths of the just," whose antiquity is immortality, and the fountain of majesty.

"Clothed with a garment down to the ankles."] In the long, that is, the priestly garment, these words very plainly deliver the flesh which was not corrupted in death, and has the priesthood through suffering.

"And He was girt about the paps with a golden girdle."] His paps are the two testaments, and the golden girdle is the choir of saints, as gold tried in the fire. Otherwise the golden girdle bound around His breast indicates the enlightened conscience, and the pure and spiritual apprehension that is given to the churches.

14. "And His head and His hairs were white as it were white wool, and as it were snow."] On the head the whiteness is shown; "but the head of Christ is God." In the white hairs is the multitude of abbots like to wool, in respect of simple sheep; to snow, in respect of the innumerable crowd of candidates taught from heaven.

"His eyes were as a flame of fire."] God's precepts are those which minister light to believers, but to unbelievers burning.

16. "And in His face was brightness as the sun."] That which He called *brightness* was the appearance of that in which He spoke to men face to face. But the glory of the *sun* is less than the glory of the Lord. Doubtless on account of its rising and setting, and rising again, that He was born and suffered and rose again, therefore the Scripture gave this similitude, likening His face to the glory of the sun.

15. "His feet were like unto yellow brass, as if burned in a furnace."] He calls the apostles His feet, who, being wrought by suffering, preached His word in the whole world; for He rightly named those by whose means the preaching went forth, feet. Whence also the prophet anticipated this, and said: "We will worship in the place where His feet have stood." Because where they first of all stood and confirmed the Church, that is, in Judea, all the saints shall assemble together, and will worship their Lord.

16. "And out of His mouth was issuing a sharp two-edged sword."] By the twice sharpened sword going

forth out of His mouth is shown, that it is He Himself who has both now declared the word of the Gospel, and previously by Moses declared the knowledge of the law to the whole world. But because from the same word, as well of the New as of the Old Testament, He will assert Himself upon the whole human race, therefore He is spoken of as two-edged. For the sword arms the soldier, the sword slays the enemy, the sword punishes the deserter. And that He might show to the apostles that He was announcing judgment, He says: "I came not to send peace, but a sword." And after He had completed His parables, He says to them: "Have ye understood all these things? And they said, We have. And He added, Therefore is every scribe instructed in the kingdom of God like unto a man that is a father of a family, bringing forth from his treasure things new and old,"—the new, the evangelical words of the apostles; the old, the precepts of the law and the prophets: and He testified that these proceeded out of His mouth. Moreover, He also says to Peter: "Go thou to the sea, and cast a hook, and take up the fish that shall first come up; and having opened its mouth, thou shalt find a *stater* (that is, two *denarii*), and thou shalt give it for me and for thee." And similarly David says by the Spirit: "God spoke once, twice I have heard the same." Because God once decreed from the beginning what shall be even to the end. Finally, as He Himself is the Judge appointed by the Father, on account of His assumption of humanity, wishing to show that men shall be judged by the word that He had declared, He says: "Think you that I will judge you at the last day? Nay, but the word," says He, "which I have spoken unto you, that shall judge you in the last day." And Paul, speaking of Antichrist to the Thessalonians, says: "Whom the Lord Jesus will slay by the breath of His mouth." And Isaiah says: "By the breath of His lips He shall slay the wicked." This, therefore, is the two-edged sword issuing out of His mouth.

15. "And His voice as it were the voice of many waters."] The many waters are understood to be many peoples, or the gift of baptism that He sent forth by the apostles, saying: "Go ye, teach all nations, baptizing them in the name of the Father, and of the Son, and of the Holy Ghost."

16. "And He had in His right hand seven stars."] He said that in His right hand He had seven stars, because the Holy Spirit of sevenfold agency was given into His power by the Father. As Peter exclaimed to the Jews: "Being at the right hand of God exalted, He hath shed forth this Spirit received from the Father, which ye both see and hear." Moreover, John the Baptist had also anticipated this, by saying to his disciples: "For God gives not the Spirit by measure *unto Him*. The Father," says he, "loves the Son, and hath given all things into His hands." Those seven stars are the seven churches, which he names in his addresses by name, and calls them to whom he wrote epistles. Not that they are themselves the only, or even the principal churches; but what he says to one, he says to all. For they are in no respect different, that on that ground anyone should prefer them to the larger number of similar small ones. In the whole world Paul taught that all the churches are arranged by sevens, that they are called seven, and that the Catholic Church is one. And first of all, indeed, that he himself also might maintain the type of seven churches, he did not exceed that number. But he wrote to the Romans, to the Corinthians, to the Galatians, to the Ephesians, to the Thessalonians, to the Philippians,

to the Colossians; afterwards he wrote to individual persons, so as not to exceed the number of seven churches. And abridging in a short space his announcement, he thus says to Timothy: "That thou may know how thou oughts' to behave thyself in the Church of the living God." We read also that this typical number is announced by the Holy Spirit by the mouth of Isaiah: "Of seven women which took hold of one man." The one man is Christ, not born of seed; but the seven women are seven churches, receiving His bread, and clothed with his apparel, who ask that their reproach should be taken away, only that His name should be called upon them. The bread is the Holy Spirit, which nourishes to eternal life, promised to them, that is, by faith. And His garments wherewith they desire to be clothed are the glory of immortality, of which Paul the apostle says: "For this corruptible must put on incorruption, and this mortal must put on immortality." Moreover, they ask that their reproach may be taken away—that is, that they may be cleansed from their sins: for the reproach is the original sin which is taken away in baptism, and they begin to be called Christian men, which is, "Let thy name be called upon us." Therefore in these seven churches, of one Catholic Church are believers, because it is one in seven by the quality of faith and election. Whether writing to them who labor in the world, and live of the frugality of their labors, and are patient, and when they see certain men in the Church wasters, and pernicious, they hear them, lest there should become dissension, he yet admonishes them by love, that in what respects their faith is deficient they should repent; or to those who dwell in cruel places among persecutors, that they should continue faithful; or to those who, under the pretext of mercy, do unlawful sins in the Church, and make them manifest to be done by others; or to those that are at ease in the Church; or to those who are negligent, and Christians only in name; or to those who are meekly instructed, that they may bravely persevere in faith; or to those who study the Scriptures, and labor to know the mysteries of their announcement, and are unwilling to do God's work that is mercy and love: to all he urges penitence, to all he declares judgment.

From the second chapter.

2. "I know thy works, and thy labor, and thy patience."] In the first epistle He speaks thus: I know that thou suffers and works, I see that thou art patient; think not that I am staying long from thee.

"And that thou canst not bear them that are evil, and who say that they are Jews and are not, and thou has found them liars, and thou hast patience for My name's sake."] All these things tend to praise, and that no small praise; and it behooves such men, and such a class, and such elected persons, by all means to be admonished, that they may not be defrauded of such privileges granted to them of God. These few things He said that He had against them.

4, 5. "And thou hast left thy first love: remember whence thou hast fallen."] He who falls, falls from a height: therefore He said *whence*: because, even to the very last, works of love must be practiced; and this is the principal commandment. Finally, unless this is done, He threatened to remove their candlestick out of its place, that is, to disperse the congregation.

6. "This thou hast also, that thou hates the deeds of the Nicolaitanes."] But because thou thyself hates those who hold the doctrines of the Nicolaitanes, thou expects praise. Moreover, to hate the works of the Nicolaitanes, which He Himself also hated, this tends to praise. But the works of the Nicolaitanes were in that time false and troublesome men, who, as ministers under the name of Nicolaus, had made for themselves a heresy, to the effect that what had been offered to idols might be exorcised and eaten, and that whoever should have committed fornication might receive peace on the eighth day. Therefore He extols those to whom He is writing; and to these men, being such and so great, He promised the tree *of life*, which is in the paradise of His God.

The following epistle unfolds the mode of life and habit of another order which follows. He proceeds to say:—

9. "I know thy tribulation and thy poverty, but thou art rich."] For He knows that with such men there are riches hidden with Him, and that they deny the blasphemy of the Jews, who say that they are Jews and are not; but they are the synagogue of Satan, since they are gathered together by Antichrist; and to them He says:—

10. "Be thou faithful unto death."] That they should continue to be faithful even unto death.

11. "He that shall overcome, shall not be hurt by the second death."] That is, he shall not be chastised in hell.

The third order of the saints shows that they are men who are strong in faith, and who are not afraid of persecution; but because even among them there are some who are inclined to unlawful associations, He says:—

14–16. "Thou hast there some who hold the doctrine of Balaam, who taught in the case of Balak that he should put a stumbling-block before the children of Israel, to eat and to commit fornication. So also hast thou them who hold the doctrine of the Nicolaitanes; but I will fight with them with the sword of my mouth."] That is, I will say what I shall command, and I will tell you what you shall do. For Balaam, with his doctrine, taught Balak to cast a stumbling-block before the eyes of the children of Israel, to eat what was sacrificed to idols, and to commit fornication,—a thing which is known to have happened of old. For he gave this advice to the king of the Moabites, and they caused stumbling to the people. Thus, says He, ye have among you those who hold such doctrine; and under the pretext of mercy, you would corrupt others.

17. "To him that overcomes I will give the hidden manna, and I will give him a white stone."] The hidden manna is immortality; the white gem is adoption to *be* the son of God; the new name written on the stone is "Christian."

The fourth class intimates the nobility of the faithful, who labor daily, and do greater works. But even among them also He shows that there are men of an easy disposition to grant unlawful peace, and to listen to new forms of prophesying; and He reproves and warns the others to whom this is not pleasing, who know the wickedness opposed to them: for which evils He purposes to bring upon the head of the faithful both sorrows and dangers; and therefore He says:—

24. "I will not put upon you any other burden."] That is, I have not given you laws, observances, and duties, which is another burden.

25, 26. "But that which ye have, hold fast until I come; and he that overcomes, to him will I give power over all peoples."] That is, him I will appoint as judge among the rest of the saints.

28. "And I will give him the morning star."] To wit, the first resurrection. He promised the morning star, which drives away the night, and announces the light, that is, the beginning of day.

From the third chapter.

The fifth class, company, or association of saints, sets forth men who are careless, and who are carrying on in the world other transactions than those which they ought—Christians only in name. And therefore He exhorts them that by any means they should be turned away from negligence, and be saved; and to this effect He says:—

2. "Be watchful, and strengthen the other things which were ready to die; for I have not found thy works perfect before God."] For it is not enough for a tree to live and to have no fruit, even as it is not enough to be called a Christian and to confess Christ, but not to have Himself in our work, that is, not to do His precepts.

The sixth class is the mode of life of the best election. The habit of saints is set forth; of those, to wit, who are lowly in the world, and unskilled in the Scriptures, and who hold the faith immoveably, and are not at all broken down by any chance, or withdrawn from the faith by any fear. Therefore He says to them:—

8. "I have set before thee an open door, because thou hast kept the word of my patience."] In such little strength.

10. "And I will keep thee from the hour of temptation."] That they may know His glory to be of this kind, that they are not indeed permitted to be given over to temptation.

12. "He that overcomes shall be made a pillar in the temple of God."] For even as a pillar is an ornament of the building, so he who perseveres shall obtain a nobility in the Church.

Moreover, the seventh association of the Church declares that they are rich men placed in positions of dignity, but believing that they are rich, among whom indeed the Scriptures are discussed in their bedchamber, while the faithful are outside; and they are understood by none, although they boast themselves, and say that they know all things,—endowed with the confidence of learning, but ceasing from its labor. And thus He says:—

15. "That they are neither cold nor hot."] That is, neither unbelieving nor believing, for they are all things to all men. And because he who is neither cold nor hot, but lukewarm, gives nausea, He says:—

16. "I will vomit thee out of My mouth."] Although nausea is hateful, still it hurts no one; so also is it with men of this kind when they have been cast forth. But because there is time of repentance, He says:—

18. "I persuade thee to buy of Me gold tried in the fire."] That is, that in whatever manner you can, you should suffer for the Lord's name tribulations and passions.

"And anoint thine eyes with eye-salve."] That what you gladly know by the Scripture, you should strive also to do the work of the same. And because, if in these ways men return out of great destruction to great repentance, they are not only useful to themselves, but they are able also to be of advantage to many, He promised them no small reward,—to sit, namely, on the throne of judgment.

From the fourth chapter.

1. "After this, I beheld, and, lo, a door was opened in heaven."] The New Testament is announced as an open door in heaven.

"And the first voice which I heard *was*, as it were, of a trumpet talking with me, saying, Come up hither."] Since the door is shown to be opened, it is manifest that previously it had been closed to men. And it was sufficiently and fully laid open when Christ ascended with His body to the Father into heaven. Moreover, the first voice which he had heard when he says that it spoke with him, without contradiction condemns those who say that one spoke in the prophets, another in the Gospel; since it is rather He Himself who comes, that is the same who spoke in the prophets. For John was of the circumcision, and all that people which had heard the announcement of the Old Testament was edified with his word.

"That very same voice," said he, "that I had heard, that said unto me, Come up hither."] That is the Spirit, whom a little before he confesses that he had seen walking as the Son of man in the midst of the golden candlesticks. And he now gathers from Him what had been foretold in similitudes by the law, and associates with this scripture all the former prophets, and opens up the Scriptures. And because our Lord invited in His own name all believers into heaven, He forthwith poured out the Holy Spirit, who should bring them to heaven. He says:—

2. "Immediately I was in the Spirit."] And since the mind of the faithful is opened by the Holy Spirit, and that is manifested to them which was also foretold to the fathers, he distinctly says:—

"And, behold, a throne was set in heaven."] The throne set: what is it but the throne of judgment and of the King?

3. "And He that sat upon the throne was, to look upon, like a jasper and a sardine stone."] Upon the throne he says that he saw the likeness of a jasper and a sardine stone. The jasper is of the color of water, the sardine of fire. These two are thence manifested to be placed as judgments upon God's tribunal until the consummation of the world, of which judgments one is already completed in the deluge of water, and the other shall be completed by fire.

"And there was a rainbow about the throne."] Moreover, the rainbow round about the throne has the same colors. The rainbow is called a bow from what the Lord spoke to Noah and to his sons, that they should not fear any further deluge in the generation of God, but fire. For thus He says: I will place my bow in the clouds, that ye may now no longer fear water, but fire.

6. "And before the throne there was, as it were, a sea of glass like to crystal."] That is the gift of baptism which He sheds forth through His Son in time of repentance, before He executes judgment. It is therefore before the throne, that is, the judgment. And when he says a sea of glass like to crystal, he shows that it is pure water, smooth, not agitated by the wind, not flowing down as on a slope, but given to be immoveable as the house of God.

"And round about the throne were four living creatures."] The four living creatures are the four Gospels.

7–10. "The first living creature was like to a lion, and the second was like to a calf, and the third had a face like to a man, and the fourth was like to a flying eagle; and they had six wings, and roundabout and within they were full of eyes; and they had no rest, saying, Holy, holy, holy, Lord Omnipotent. And the four and twenty elders, falling down before the throne, adored God."] The four and twenty elders are the twenty-four books of the prophets and of the law, which give testimonies of the judgment. Moreover, also, they are the twenty-four fathers—twelve apostles and twelve patriarchs. And in that the living creatures are different in appearance, this is the reason: the living creature like to a lion designates Mark, in whom is heard the voice of the lion roaring in the desert. And in the figure of a man, Matthew strives to declare to us the genealogy of Mary, from whom Christ took flesh. Therefore, in enumerating from Abraham to David, and thence to Joseph, he spoke of Him as if of a man: therefore his announcement sets forth the image of a man. Luke, in narrating the priesthood of Zacharias as he offers a sacrifice for the people, and the angel that appears to him with respect of the priesthood, and the victim in the same description bore the likeness of a calf. John the evangelist, like to an eagle hastening on uplifted wings to greater heights, argues about the Word of God. Mark, therefore, as an evangelist thus beginning, "The beginning of the Gospel of Jesus Christ, as it is written in Isaiah the prophet;" The voice of one crying in the wilderness,"—has the effigy of a lion. And Matthew, "The book of the generation of Jesus Christ, the son of David, the son of Abraham:"168 this is the form of a man. But Luke said,

"There was a priest, by name Zachariah, of the course of Abia, and his wife was of the daughters of Aaron:" this is the likeness of a calf. But John, when he begins, "In the beginning was the Word, and the Word was with God, and the Word was God," sets forth the likeness of a flying eagle. Moreover, not only do the evangelists express their four similitudes in their *respective* openings of the Gospels, but also the Word itself of God the Father Omnipotent, which is His Son our Lord Jesus Christ, bears the same likeness in the time of His advent. When He preaches to us, He is, as it were, a lion and a lion's whelp. And when for man's salvation He was made man to overcome death, and to set all men free, and that He offered Himself a victim to the Father on our behalf, He was called a calf. And that He overcame death and ascended into the heavens, extending His wings and protecting His people, He was named a flying eagle. Therefore these announcements, although they are four, yet are one, because it proceeded from one mouth. Even as the river in paradise, although it is one, was divided into four heads. Moreover, that for the announcement of the New Testament those living creatures had eyes within and without, shows the spiritual providence which both looks into the secrets of the heart, and beholds the things which are coming after that are within and without.

8. "Six wings."] These are the testimonies of the books of the Old Testament. Thus, twenty and four make as many as there are elders sitting upon the thrones. But as an animal cannot fly unless it have wings, so, too, the announcement of the New Testament gains no faith unless it have the fore-announced testimonies of the Old Testament, by which it is lifted from the earth, and flies. For in every case, what has been told before, and is

afterwards found to have happened, that begets an undoubting faith. Again, also, if wings be not attached to the living creatures, they have nothing whence they may draw their life. For unless what the prophets foretold had been consummated in Christ, their preaching was vain. For the Catholic Church holds those things which were both before predicted and afterwards accomplished. And it flies, because the living animal is reasonably lifted up from the earth. But to heretics who do not avail themselves of the prophetic testimony, to them also there are present living creatures; but they do not fly, because they are of the earth. And to the Jews who do *not* receive the announcement of the New Testament there are present wings; but they do not fly, that is, they bring a vain prophesying to men, not adjusting facts to their words. And the books of the Old Testament that are received are twenty-four, which you will find in the epitomes of Theodore. But, moreover (as we have said), four and twenty elders, patriarchs and apostles, are to judge His people. For to the apostles, when they asked, saying, "We have forsaken all that we had, and followed Thee: what shall we have?" our Lord replied, "When the Son of man shall sit upon the throne of His glory, ye also shall sit upon twelve thrones, judging the twelve tribes of Israel." But of the fathers also who should judge, says the patriarch Jacob, "Dan also himself shall judge his people among his brethren, even as one of the tribes in Israel."

5. "And from the throne proceeded lightnings, and voices, and thunders, and seven torches of fire burning."] And the lightnings, and voices, and thunders proceeding from the throne of God, and the seven torches of fire burning, signify announcements, and promises of adoption, and threatening. For lightnings signify the

Lord's advent, and the voices the announcements of the New Testament, and the thunders, that the words are from heaven. The burning torches of fire *signify* the gift of the Holy Spirit, that it is given by the wood of the passion. And when these things were doing, he says that all the elders fell down and adored the Lord; while the living creatures—that is, of course, the actions recorded in the Gospels and the teaching of the Lord—gave Him glory and honor. In that they had fulfilled the word that had been previously foretold by them, they worthily and with reason exult, feeling that they have ministered the mysteries and the word of the Lord. Finally, also, because He had come who should remove death, and who alone was worthy to take the crown of immortality, all for the glory of His most excellent doing had crowns.

10. "And they cast their crowns under His feet."] That is, on account of the eminent glory of Christ's victory, they cast all their victories under His feet. This is what in the Gospel the Holy Spirit consummated by showing, For when about finally to suffer, our Lord had come to Jerusalem, and the people had gone forth to meet Him, some strewed the road with palm branches cut down, others threw down their garments, doubtless these were setting forth two peoples—the one of the patriarchs, the other of the prophets; that is to say, of the great men who had any kind of palms of their victories against sin, and cast them under the feet of Christ, the victor of all. And the palm and the crown signify the same things, and these are not given save to the victor.

From the fifth chapter.

1. "And I saw in the right hand of Him that sat upon the throne, a book written within and without, sealed with seven seals."] This book signifies the Old Testament, which has been given into the hands of our Lord Jesus Christ, who received from the Father judgment.

2, 3. "And I saw an angel full of strength proclaiming with a loud voice, Who is worthy to open the book, and to loose the seals thereof? And no one was found worthy, neither in the earth nor under the earth, to open the book."] Now to open the book is to overcome death for man.

4. "There was none found worthy to do this."] Neither among the angels of heaven, nor among men in earth, nor among the souls of the saints in rest, save Christ the Son of God alone, whom he says that he saw as a Lamb standing as it were slain, having seven horns. What had not been then announced, and what the law had contemplated for Him by its various oblations and sacrifices, it behooved Himself to fulfil. And because He Himself was the testator, who had overcome death, it was just that Himself should be appointed the Lord's heir, that He should possess the substance of the dying man, that is, the human members.

5. "Lo, the Lion of the tribe of Judah, the root of David, hath prevailed."] We read in Genesis that this lion of the tribe of Judah hath conquered, when the patriarch Jacob says, "Judah, thy brethren shall praise thee; thou hast lain down and slept, and hast risen up again as a lion, and as a lion's whelp." For He is called a lion for the overcoming of death; but for the suffering for men He was led as a lamb to the slaughter. But because He

overcame death, and anticipated the duty of the executioner, He was called as it were slain. He therefore opens and seals again the testament, which He Himself had sealed. The legislator Moses intimating this, that it behooved Him to be sealed and concealed, even to the advent of His passion, veiled his face, and so spoke to the people; showing that the words of his announcement were veiled even to the advent of His time. For he himself, when he had read to the people, having taken the wool purpled with the blood of the calf, with water sprinkled the whole people, saying, "This is the blood of His testament who hath purified you." It should therefore be observed that the Man is accurately announced, and that all things combine into one. For it is not sufficient that that law is spoken of, but it is named as a testament. For no law is called a testament, nor is anything else called a testament, save what persons make who are about to die. And whatever is within the testament is sealed, even to the day of the testator's death. Therefore it is with reason that it is only sealed by the Lamb slain, who, as it were a lion, has broken death in pieces, and has fulfilled what had been foretold; and has delivered man, that is, the flesh, from death, and has received as a possession the substance of the dying person, that is, of the human members; that as by one body all men had fallen under the obligation of its death, also by one body all believers should be born again unto life, and rise again. Reasonably, therefore, His face is opened and unveiled to Moses; and therefore He is called Apocalypse, Revelation. For now His book is unsealed—now the offered victims are perceived—now the fabrication of the priestly chrism; moreover the testimonies are openly understood.

8, 9. "Twenty-four elders and four living creatures, having harps and phials, and singing a new song."] The proclamation of the Old Testament associated with the New, points out the Christian people singing a new song, that is, bearing their confession publicly. It is a new thing that the Son of God should become man. It is a new thing to ascend into the heavens with a body. It is a new thing to give remission of sins to men. It is a new thing for men to be sealed with the Holy Spirit. It is a new thing to receive the priesthood of sacred observance, and to look for a kingdom of unbounded promise. The harp, and the chord stretched on its wooden frame, signifies the flesh of Christ linked with the wood of the passion. The phial signifies *the* Confession, and the race of the new Priesthood. But it is the praise of many angels, yea, of all, the salvation of all, and the testimony of the universal creation, bringing to our Lord thanksgiving for the deliverance of men from the destruction of death. The unsealing of the seals, as we have said, is the opening of the Old Testament, and the foretelling of the preachers of things to come in the last times, which, although the prophetic Scripture speaks by single seals, yet by all the seals opened at once, prophecy takes its rank.

From the sixth chapter.

1, 2. "And when the Lamb had opened one of the seven seals, I saw, and heard one of the four living creatures saying, Come and see. And, lo, a white horse, and He who sat upon him had a bow."] The first seal being opened, he says that he saw a white horse, and a crowned horseman having a bow. For this was at first done by Himself. For after the Lord ascended into heaven and opened all things, He sent the Holy Spirit, whose words the preachers sent forth as arrows reaching to the human heart, that they might overcome unbelief. And the crown on the head is promised to the preachers by the Holy Spirit. The other three horses very plainly signify the wars, famines, and pestilences announced by our Lord in the Gospel. And thus he says that one of the four living creatures said (because all four are one), "Come and see." "Come" is said to him that is invited to faith; "see" is said to him who saw not. Therefore the white horse is the word of preaching with the Holy Spirit sent into the world. For the Lord says, "This Gospel shall be preached throughout the whole world for a testimony to all nations, and then shall come the end."

3, 4. "And when He had opened the second seal, I heard the second living creature saying, Come and see. And there went out another horse that was red, and to him that sat upon him was given a great sword."] The red horse, and he that sat upon him, having a sword, signify the coming wars, as we read in the Gospel: "For nation shall rise against nation, and kingdom against kingdom; and there shall be great earthquakes in *divers* places." This is the ruddy horse.

5. "And when He had opened the third seal, I heard the third living creature saying, Come and see. And, lo, a black horse; and he who sat upon it had a balance in his hand."] The black horse signifies famine, for the Lord says, "There shall be famines in *divers* places;" but the word is specially extended to the times of Antichrist, when there shall be a great famine, and when all shall be injured. Moreover, the balance in the hand is the examining scales, wherein He might show forth the merits of every individual. He then says:—

6. "Hurt not the wine and the oil."] That is, strike not the spiritual man with thy inflictions. This is the black horse.

7, 8. "And when He had opened the fourth seal, I heard the fourth living creature saying, Come and see. And, lo, a pale horse; and he who sat upon him was named Death."] For the pale horse and he who sat upon him bore the name of Death. These same things also the Lord had promised among the rest of the coming destructions—great pestilences and deaths; since, moreover, he says:—

"And hell followed him."] That is, it was waiting for the devouring of many unrighteous souls. This is the pale horse.

9. "And when He had opened the fifth seal, I saw under the altar the souls of them that were slain."] He relates that he saw under the altar of God, that is, under the earth, the souls of them that were slain. For both heaven and earth are called God's altar, as said the law, commanding in the symbolical form of the truth two altars to be made,—a golden one within, and a brazen one without. But we perceive that the golden altar is thus called heaven, by the testimony that our Lord bears to it; for He says, "When thou brings thy gift to the altar" (assuredly our gifts are the prayers which we offer), "and there remembers that thy brother hath ought against thee, leave there thy gift before the altar." Assuredly prayers ascend to heaven. Therefore heaven is understood to be the golden altar which was within; for the priests also were accustomed to enter once in the year—as they who had the anointing—to the golden altar, the Holy Spirit signifying that Christ should do this once for all. As the golden altar is acknowledged to be heaven, so also by the

brazen altar is understood the earth, under which is the Hades,—a region withdrawn from punishments and fires, and a place of repose for the saints, wherein indeed the righteous are seen and heard by the wicked, but they cannot be carried across to them. He who sees all things would have us to know that these saints, therefore—that is, the souls of the slain—are asking for vengeance for their blood, that is, of their body, from those that dwell upon the earth; but because in the last time, moreover, the reward of the saints will be perpetual, and the condemnation of the wicked shall come, it was told them to wait. And for a solace to their body, there were given unto each of them white robes. They received, says he, white robes, that is, the gift of the Holy Spirit.

12. "And I saw, when he had opened the sixth seal, there was a great earthquake."] In the sixth seal, then, was a great earthquake: this is that very last persecution.

"And the sun became black as sackcloth of hair."] The sun becomes as sackcloth; that is, the brightness of doctrine will be obscured by unbelievers.

"And the entire moon became as blood."] By the moon of blood is set forth the Church of the saints as pouring out her blood for Christ.

13. "And the stars fell to the earth."] The falling of the stars are the faithful who are troubled for Christ's sake.

"Even as a fig-tree casted her untimely figs."] The fig-tree, when shaken, loses its untimely figs—when men are separated from the Church by persecution.

14. "And the heaven withdrew as a scroll that is rolled up."] For the heaven to be rolled away, that is, that the Church shall be taken away.

"And every mountain and the islands were moved from their places."] Mountains and islands removed from their places intimate that in the last persecution all men departed from their places; that is, that the good will be removed, seeking to avoid the persecution.

From the seventh chapter.

2. "And I saw another angel ascending from the east, having the seal of the living God."] He speaks of Elias the prophet, who is the precursor of the times of Antichrist, for the restoration and establishment of the churches from the great and intolerable persecution. We read that these things are predicted in the opening of the Old and New Testament; for He says by Malachi: "Lo, I will send to you Elias the Tishbite, to turn the hearts of the fathers to the children, according to the time of calling, to recall the Jews to the faith of the people that succeed them." And to that end He shows, as we have said, that the number of those that shall believe, of the Jews and of the nations, is a great multitude which no man was able to number. Moreover, we read in the Gospel that the prayers of the Church are sent from heaven by an angel, and that they are received against wrath, and that the kingdom of Antichrist is cast out and extinguished by holy angels; for He says: "Pray that ye enter not into temptation: for there shall be a great affliction, such as has not been from the beginning of the world; and except the Lord had shortened those days, no flesh should be saved." Therefore He shall send these seven great archangels to smite the kingdom of Antichrist; for He Himself also thus said: "Then the Son of man shall send His messengers; and they shall gather together His

elect from the four corners of the wind, from the one end of heaven even to the other end thereof." For, moreover, He previously says by the prophet: "Then shall there be peace for our land, when there shall arise in it seven shepherds and eight attacks of men; and they shall encircle Assur," that is, Antichrist, "in the trench of Nimrod," that is, in the nation of the devil, by the spirit of the Church. Similarly when the keepers of the house shall be moved. Moreover, the Lord Himself, in the parable to the apostles, when the laborers had come to Him and said, "Lord, did not we sow good seed in Thy field? Whence, then, hath it tares? Answered them, An enemy hath done this. And they said to Him, Lord, wilt Thou, then, that we go and root them up? And He said, Nay, but let both grow together until the harvest; and in the time of the harvest I will say to the reapers, that they gather the tares and make bundles of them, and burn them with fire everlasting, but that they gather the wheat into my barns." The Apocalypse here shows, therefore, that these reapers, and shepherds, and laborers, are the angels. And the trumpet is the word of power. And although the same thing recurs in the phials, still it is not said as if it occurred twice, but because what is decreed by the Lord to happen shall be once for all; for this cause it is said twice. What, therefore, He said too little in the trumpets, is here found in the phials. We must not regard the order of what is said, because frequently the Holy Spirit, when He has traversed even to the end of the last times, returns again to the same times, and fills up what He had *before* failed to say. Nor must we look for order in the Apocalypse; but we must follow the meaning of those things which are prophesied. Therefore in the trumpets and phials is signified either the desolation of the plagues that are sent upon the earth, or the madness of Antichrist himself, or the cutting off of the peoples, or the diversity of the plagues, or the hope in the kingdom of the saints, or the ruin of states, or the great overthrow of Babylon, that is, the Roman state.

9. "After this I beheld, and, lo, a great multitude, which no man was able to number, of every nation, tribe, and people, and tongue, clothed with white robes."] What the great multitude out of every tribe implies, is to show the number of the elect out of all believers, who, being cleansed by baptism in the blood of the Lamb, have made their robes white, keeping the grace which they have received.

From the eighth chapter.

1. "And when He had opened the seventh seal, there was silence in heaven for about half an hour."] Whereby is signified the beginning of everlasting rest; but it is described as partial, because the silence being interrupted, he repeats it in order. For if the silence had continued, here would be an end of his narrative.

13. "And I saw an angel flying through the midst of heaven."] By the angel flying through the midst of heaven is signified the Holy Spirit bearing witness in two of the prophets that a great wrath of plagues was imminent. If by any means, even in the last times, anyone should be willing to be converted, any one might even still be saved.

From the ninth chapter.

13, 14. "And I heard a voice from the four horns of the golden altar which is in the presence of God, saying to the sixth angel which had the trumpet, Loose the four angels."] That is, the four corners of the earth which hold the four winds.

"Which are bound in the great river Euphrates."] By the corners of the earth, or the four winds across the river Euphrates, are *meant* four nations, because to every nation is sent an angel; as said the law, "He determined them by the number of the angels of God," until the number of the saints should be filled up. They do not overpass their bounds, because at the last they shall come with Antichrist.

From the tenth chapter.

1, 2. "I saw another mighty angel coming down from heaven, clothed with a cloud; and a rainbow was upon his head, and his face was as it were the sun, and his feet as pillars of fire: and he had in his hand an open book: and he set his right foot upon the sea, and his left foot upon the earth."] He signifies that that mighty angel who, he says, descended from heaven, clothed with a cloud, is our Lord, as we have above narrated.

"His face was as it were the sun."] That is, with respect to the resurrection.

"Upon his head was a rainbow."] He points to the judgment which is executed by Him, or shall be.

"An open book."] A revelation of works in the future judgment, or the Apocalypse which John received.

"His feet,"] as we have said above, are the apostles. For that both things in sea and land are trodden under foot by Him, signifies that all things are placed under His feet. Moreover, he calls Him an angel, that is, a messenger, to wit, of the Father; for He is called the Messenger of great counsel. He says also that He cried with a loud voice. The great voice is to tell the words of the Omnipotent God of heaven to men, and to bear witness that after penitence is closed there will be no hope subsequently.

3. "Seven thunders uttered their voices."] The seven thunders uttering their voices signify the Holy Spirit of sevenfold power, who through the prophets announced all things to come, and by His voice John gave his testimony in the world; but because he says that he was about to write the things which the thunders had uttered, that is, whatever things had been obscure in the announcements of the Old Testament; he is forbidden to write them, but he was charged to leave them sealed, because he is an apostle, nor was it fitting that the grace of the subsequent stage should be given in the first. "The time," says he, "is at hand."

For the apostles, by powers, by signs, by portents, and by mighty works, have overcome unbelief. After them there is now given to the same completed Churches the comfort of having the prophetic Scriptures subsequently interpreted, for I said that after *the apostles* there would be interpreting prophets.

For the apostle says: "And he placed in the Church indeed, first, apostles; secondly, prophets; thirdly, teachers," and the rest. And in another place he says: "Let the prophets speak two or three, and let the others judge." And he says: "Every woman that prayed or prophesied with her head uncovered, dishonored her head." And when he says, "Let the prophets speak two or three, and let the others judge," he is not speaking in respect of the Catholic prophecy of things unheard and unknown, but of things both announced and known. But let them judge whether or not the interpretation is consistent with the testimonies of the prophetic utterance. It is plain, therefore, that to John, armed as he was with superior virtue, this was not necessary, although the body of Christ, which is the Church, adorned with His members, ought to respond to its position.

10. "I took the book from the hand of the angel, and ate it up."] To take the book and eat it up, is, when exhibition of a thing is made to one, to commit it to memory.

"And it was in my mouth as sweet as honey."] To be sweet in the mouth is the reward of the preaching of the speaker, and is most pleasant to the hearers; but it is most bitter both to those that announce it, and to those that persevere in its commandments through suffering.

11. "And He says unto me, Thou must again prophesy to the peoples, and to the tongues, and to the nations, and to many kings."] He says this, because when John said these things he was in the island of Patmos, condemned to the labor of the mines by Cæsar Domitian. There, therefore, he saw the Apocalypse; and when grown old, he thought that he should at length receive his quittance by suffering, Domitian being killed, all his judgments were discharged. And John being dismissed from the mines, thus subsequently delivered the same Apocalypse which he had received from God. This, therefore, is what He says: Thou must again prophesy to

all nations, because thou sees the crowds of Antichrist rise up; and against them other crowds shall stand, and they shall fall by the sword on the one side and on the other.

From the eleventh chapter.

1. "And there was shown unto me a reed like unto a rod: and the angel stood, saying, Rise, and measure the temple of God, and the altar, and them that worship therein."] A reed was shown like to a rod. This itself is the Apocalypse which he subsequently exhibited to the churches; for the Gospel of the complete faith he subsequently wrote for the sake of our salvation. For when Valentinus, and Cerinthus, and Ebion, and others of the school of Satan, were scattered abroad throughout the world, there assembled together to him from the neighboring provinces all the bishops, and compelled him himself also to draw up his testimony. Moreover, we say that the measure of God's temple is the command of God to confess the Father Almighty, and that His Son Christ was begotten by the Father before the beginning of the world, and was made man in very soul and flesh, both of them having overcome misery and death; and that, when received with His body into heaven by the Father, He shed forth the Holy Spirit, the gift and pledge of immortality, that He was announced by the prophets, He was described by the law, He was God's hand, and the Word of the Father from God, Lord over all, and founder of the world: this is the reed and the measure of faith; and no one worships the holy altar save he who confesses this faith.

2. "The court which is within the temple leave out."] The space which is called the court is the empty

altar within the walls: these being such as were not necessary, he commanded to be ejected from the Church.

"It is given to be trodden down by the Gentiles."] That is, to the men of this world, that it may be trodden under foot by the nations, or with the nations. Then he repeats about the destruction and slaughter of the last time, and says:—

3. "They shall tread the holy city down for forty and two months; and I will give to my two witnesses, and they shall predict a thousand two hundred and threescore days clothed in sackcloth."] That is, three years and six months: these make forty-two months. Therefore their preaching is three years and six months, and the kingdom of Antichrist as much again.

5. "If any man will hurt them, fire proceeded out of their mouth, and devoured their enemies."] That fire proceeded out of the mouth of those prophets against the adversaries, bespeaks the power of the world. For all afflictions, however many there are, shall be sent by their messengers in their word. Many think that there is Elisha, or Moses, with Elijah; but both of these died; while the death of Elijah is not heard of, with whom all our ancients have believed that it was Jeremiah. For even the very word spoken to him testifies to him, saying, "Before I formed thee in the belly I knew thee; and before thou camest forth out of the womb I sanctified thee, and I ordained thee a prophet unto the nations." But he was not a prophet unto the nations; and thus the truthful word of God makes it necessary, which it has promised to set forth, that he should be a prophet to the nations.

4. "These are the two candlesticks standing before the Lord of the earth."] These two candlesticks and two olive trees He has to this end spoken of, and admonished

you that if, when you have read of them elsewhere, you have not understood, you may understand here. For in Zechariah, one of the twelve prophets, it is thus written: "These are the two olive trees and two candlesticks which stand in the presence of the Lord of the earth;" that is, they are in paradise. Also, in another sense, standing in the presence of the lord of the earth, that is, in the presence of Antichrist. Therefore they must be slain by Antichrist.

7. "And the beast which ascended from the abyss."] After many plagues completed in the world, in the end he says that a beast ascended from the abyss. But that he shall ascend from the abyss is proved by many testimonies; for he says in the thirty-first chapter of Ezekiel: "Behold, Assur was a cypress in Mount Lebanon." Assur, deeply rooted, was a lofty and branching cypress—that is, a numerous people—in Mount Lebanon, in the kingdom of kingdoms, that is, of the Romans. Moreover, that he says he was beautiful in offshoots, he says he was strong in armies. The water, he says, shall nourish him, that is, the many thousands of men which were subjected to him; and the abyss increased him, that is, belched him forth. For even Isaiah speaks almost in the same words; moreover, that he was in the kingdom of the Romans, and that he was among the Cæsars. The Apostle Paul also bears witness, for he says to the Thessalonians: "Let him who now restrained restrain, until he be taken out of the way; and then shall appear that Wicked One, even he whose coming is after the working of Satan, with signs and lying wonders." And that they might know that he should come who then was the prince, he added: "He already endeavors after the secret of mischief"—that is, the mischief which he is

about to do he strives to do secretly; but he is not raised up by his own power, nor by that of his father, but by command of God, of which thing Paul says in the same passage: "For this cause, because they have not received the love of God, He will send upon them a spirit of error, that they all may be persuaded of a lie, who have not been persuaded of the truth." And Isaiah said: "While they waited for the light, darkness arose upon them." Therefore the Apocalypse sets forth that these prophets are killed by the same, and on the fourth day rise again, that none might be found equal to God.

8. "And their dead bodies shall lie in the streets of the great city, which spiritually is called Sodom and Egypt."] But He calls Jerusalem Sodom and Egypt, since it had become the heaping up of the persecuting people. Therefore it behooves us diligently, and with the utmost care, to follow the prophetic announcement, and to understand what the Spirit from the Father both announces and anticipates, and how, when He has gone forward to the last times, He again repeats the former ones. And now, what He will do once for all, He sometimes sets forth as if it were done; and unless you understand this, as sometimes done, and sometimes as about to be done, you will fall into a great confusion. Therefore the interpretation of the following sayings has shown therein, that not the order of the reading, but the order of the discourse, must be understood.

19. "And the temple of God was opened which is in heaven."] The temple opened is a manifestation of our Lord. For the temple of God is the Son, as He Himself says: "Destroy this temple, and in three days I will raise it up." And when the Jews said, "Forty and six years was

this temple in building," the evangelist says, "He spoke of the temple of His body."

"And there was seen in His temple the ark of the Lord's testament."] The preaching of the Gospel and the forgiveness of sins, and all the gifts whatever that came with Him, he says, appeared therein.

From the twelfth chapter.

1. "And there was seen a great sign in heaven. A woman clothed with the sun, and the moon under her feet, and on her head a crown of twelve stars. And being with child, she cried out travailing, and bearing torments that she might bring forth."] The woman clothed with the sun, and having the moon under her feet, and wearing a crown of twelve stars upon her head, and travailing in her pains, is the ancient Church of fathers, and prophets, and saints, and apostles, which had the groans and torments of its longing until it saw that Christ, the fruit of its people according to the flesh long promised to it, had taken flesh out of the selfsame people. Moreover, being clothed with the sun intimates the hope of resurrection and the glory of the promise. And the moon intimates the fall of the bodies of the saints under the obligation of death, which never can fail. For even as life is diminished, so also it is increased. Nor is the hope of those that sleep extinguished absolutely, as some think, but they have in their darkness a light such as the moon. And the crown of twelve stars signifies the choir of fathers, according to the fleshly birth, of whom Christ was to take flesh.

3. "And there appeared another sign in heaven; and behold a red dragon, having seven heads."] Now, that

he says that this dragon was of a red color—that is, of a purple color— the result of his work gave him such a color. For from the beginning (as the Lord says) he was a murderer; and he has oppressed the whole of the human race, not so much by the obligation of death, as, moreover, by the various forms of destruction and fatal mischiefs. His seven heads were the seven kings of the Romans, of whom also is Antichrist, as we have said above.

"And ten horns."] He says that the ten kings in the latest times are the same as these, as we shall more fully set forth there.

4. "And his tail drew the third part of the stars of heaven, and cast them upon the earth."] Now, that he says that the dragon's tail drew the third part of the stars of heaven, this may be taken in two ways. For many think that he may be able to seduce the third part of the men who believe. But it should more truly be understood, that of the angels that were subject to him, since he was still a prince when he descended from his estate, he seduced the third part; therefore what we said above, the Apocalypse says.

"And the dragon stood before the woman who was beginning to bring forth, that, when she had brought forth, he might devour her child."] The red dragon standing and desiring to devour her child when she had brought him forth, is the devil,—to wit, the traitor angel, who thought that the perishing of all men would be alike by death; but He, who was not born of seed, owed nothing to death: wherefore he could not devour Him—that is, detain Him in death—for on the third day He rose again. Finally, also, and before He suffered, he approached to tempt Him as man; but when he found that He was not what he thought

Him to be, he departed from Him, even till the time. Whence it is here said:—

5. "And she brought forth a son, who begins to rule all nations with a rod of iron."] The rod of iron is the sword of persecution.

"I saw that all men withdrew from his abodes."] That is, the good will be removed, flying from persecution.

"And her son was caught up to God, and to His throne."] We read also in the Acts of the Apostles that He was caught up to God's throne, just as speaking with the disciples He was caught up to heaven.

6. "But the woman fled into the wilderness, and there were given to her two great eagle's wings."] The aid of the great eagle's wings—to wit, the gift of prophets—was given to that Catholic Church, whence in the last times a hundred and forty-four thousands of men should believe on the preaching of Elias; but, moreover, he here says that the rest of the people should be found alive on the coming of the Lord. And the Lord says in the Gospel: "Then let them which are in Judea flee to the mountains;" that is, as many as should be gathered together in Judea, let them go to that place which they have ready, and let them be supported there for three years and six months from the presence of the devil.

14. "Two great wings"] are the two prophets—Elias, and the prophet who shall be with him.

15. "And the serpent cast out of his mouth after the woman water as a flood, that he might carry her away with the flood."] He signifies by the water which the serpent cast out of his mouth, the people who at his command would persecute her.

16. "And the earth helped the woman, and opened her mouth, and swallowed up the flood which the dragon cast out of his mouth."] That the earth opened her month and swallowed up the waters, sets forth the vengeance for the present troubles. Although, therefore, it may signify this woman bringing forth, it shows her afterwards flying when her offspring is brought forth, because both things did not happen at one time; for we know that Christ was born, but that the time should arrive that she should flee from the face of the serpent: (we do not know) that this has happened as yet. Then he says:—

7–9. "There was a battle in heaven: Michael and his angels fought with the dragon; and the dragon warred, and his angels, and they prevailed not; nor was their place found any more in heaven. And that great dragon was cast forth, that old serpent: he was cast forth into the earth."] This is the beginning of Antichrist; yet previously Elias must prophesy, and there must be times of peace. And afterwards, when the three years and six months are completed in the preaching of Elias, he also must be cast down from heaven, where up till that time he had had the power of ascending; and all the apostate angels, as well as Antichrist, must be roused up from hell. Paul the apostle says: "Except there comes a falling away first, and the man of sin shall appear, the son of perdition; and the adversary who exalted himself above all which is called God, or which is worshipped."

From the thirteenth chapter.

1. "And I saw a beast rising up from the sea, like unto a leopard."] This signifies the kingdom of that time of Antichrist, and the people mingled with the variety of nations.

2. "His feet were as the feet of a bear."] A strong and most unclean beast, the feet are to be understood as his leaders.

"And his mouth as the mouth of a lion."] That is, his mouth armed for blood is his bidding, and a tongue which will proceed to nothing else than to the shedding of blood.

* * * * * * * *

18. "His number is the name of a man, and his number is Six hundred threescore and six."] As they have it reckoned from the Greek characters, they thus find it among many to be τειταν, for τειταν has this number, which the Gentiles call Sol and Phoebus; and it is reckoned in Greek thus: τ three hundred, ε five, ι ten, τ three hundred, α one, ν fifty,—which taken together become six hundred and sixty-six. For as far as belongs to the Greek letters, they fill up this number and name; which name if you wish to turn into Latin, it is understood by the antiphrase DICLUX, which letters are reckoned in this manner: since D figures five hundred, I one, C a hundred, L fifty, V five, X ten,—which by the reckoning up of the letters makes similarly six hundred and sixty-six, that is, what in Greek gives τειταν, to wit, what in Latin is called DICLUX; by which name, expressed by antiphrases, we understand Antichrist, who, although he

be cut off from the supernal light, and deprived thereof, yet transforms himself into an angel of light, daring to call himself light. Moreover, we find in a certain Greek codex αντεμος, which letters being reckoned up, you will find to give the number as above: α one, ν fifty, τ three hundred, ε five, μ forty, ο seventy, ς two hundred,—which together makes six hundred and sixty-six, according to the Greeks. Moreover, there is another name in Gothic of him, which will be evident of itself, that is, γενσήρικος, which in the same way you will reckon in Greek letters: γ three, ε five, ν fifty, σ two hundred, η eight, ρ a hundred, ι ten, κ twenty, ο seventy, ς also two hundred, which, as has been said above, make six hundred and sixty-six.

11. "And I saw another beast coming up out of the earth."] He is speaking of the great and false prophet who is to do signs, and portents, and falsehoods before him in the presence of men.

"And he had two horns like a lamb—that is, the appearance within of a man—and he spoke like a dragon."] But the devil speaks full of malice; for he shall do these things in the presence of men, so that even the dead appear to rise again.

13. "And he shall make fire come down from heaven in the sight of men."] Yes (as I also have said), in the sight of men. Magicians do these things, by the aid of the apostate angels, even to this day. He shall cause also that a golden image of Antichrist shall be placed in the temple at Jerusalem, and that the apostate angel should enter, and thence utter voices and oracles. Moreover, he himself shall contrive that his servants and children should receive as a mark on their foreheads, or on their right hands, the number of his name, lest anyone should buy or sell them. Daniel had previously predicted his

contempt and provocation of God. "And he shall place," says he, "his temple within Samaria, upon the illustrious and holy mountain that is at Jerusalem, an image such as Nebuchadnezzar had made." Thence here he places, and by and by here he renews, that of which the Lord, admonishing His churches concerning the last times and their dangers, says: "But when ye shall see the contempt which is spoken of by Daniel the prophet standing in the holy place, let him who reads understand." It is called a contempt when God is provoked, because idols are worshipped instead of God, or when the dogma of heretics is introduced in the churches. But it is a turning away because steadfast men, seduced by false signs and portents, are turned away from their salvation.

From the fourteenth chapter.

6. "And I saw an angel flying through the midst of heaven."] The angel flying through the midst of heaven, whom he says that he saw, we have already treated of above, as being the same Elias who anticipates the kingdom of Antichrist in his prophecy.

8. "And another angel following him."] The other angel following, he speaks of as the same prophet who is the associate of his prophesying. But that he says,—

15. "Thrust in thy sharp sickle, and gather in the grapes of the vine,"] he signifies it of the nations that should perish on the advent of the Lord. And indeed in many forms he shows this same thing, as if to the dry harvest, and the seed for the coming of the Lord, and the consummation of the world, and the kingdom of Christ, and the future appearance of the kingdom of the blessed.

19, 20. "And the angel thrust in the sickle, and reaped the vine of the earth, and cast it into the wine-press of the wrath of God. And the wine-press of His fury was trodden down without the city."] In that he says that it was cast into the wine-press of the wrath of God, and trodden down without the city, the treading of the wine-press is the retribution on the sinner.

"And blood went out from the wine-press, even unto the horse-bridles."] The vengeance of shed blood as was before predicted, "In blood thou hast sinned, and blood shall follow thee."

"For a thousand and six hundred furlongs."] That is, through all the four parts of the world: for there is a quadrate put together by fours, as in four faces and four appearances, and wheels by fours; for forty times four is one thousand six hundred. Repeating the same persecution, the Apocalypse says:—

From the fifteenth chapter.

1. "And I saw another great and wonderful sign, seven angels having the seven last plagues; for in them is completed the indignation of God."] For the wrath of God always strikes the obstinate people with seven plagues, that is, perfectly, as it is said in Leviticus; and these shall be in the last time, when the Church shall have gone out of the midst.

2. "Standing upon the sea of glass, having harps."] That is, that they stood steadfastly in the faith upon their baptism, and having their confession in their mouth, that they shall exult in the kingdom before God. But let us return to what is set before us.

From the seventeenth chapter.

1–6. "There came one of the seven angels, which have the seven bowls, and spoke with me, saying, Come, I will show thee the judgment of that great whore who sits upon many waters. And I saw the woman drunk with the blood of the saints, and with the blood of the martyrs."] The decrees of that senate are always accomplished against all, contrary to the preaching of the true faith; and now already mercy being cast aside, itself here gave the decree among all nations.

3. "And I saw the woman herself sitting upon the scarlet-colored beast, full of names of blasphemy."] But to sit upon the scarlet beast, the author of murders, is the image of the devil. Where also *is treated* of his captivity, concerning which we have fully considered. I remember, indeed, that this is called Babylon also in the Apocalypse, on account of confusion; and in Isaiah also; and Ezekiel called it Sodom. In fine, if you compare what is said against Sodom, and what Isaiah says against Babylon, and what the Apocalypse says, you will find that they are all one.

9. "The seven heads are the seven hills, on which the woman sits."] That is, the city of Rome.

10. "And there are seven kings: five have fallen, and one is, and the other is not yet come; and when he is come, he will be for a short time."] The time must be understood in which the written Apocalypse was published, since then reigned Cæsar Domitian; but before him had been Titus his brother, and Vespasian, Otho, Vitellius, and Galba. These are the five who have fallen. One remains, under whom the Apocalypse was written—Domitian, to wit. "The other has not yet come," speaks of

Nerva; "and when he is come, he will be for a short time," for he did not complete the period of two years.

11. "And the beast which thou saw is of the seven."] Since before those kings Nero reigned.

"And he is the eighth."] He says only when this beast shall come, reckon it the eighth place, since in that is the completion. He added:—

"And shall go into perdition."] For that ten kings received royal power when he shall move from the east, he says. He shall be sent from the city of Rome with his armies. And Daniel sets forth the ten horns and the ten diadems. And that these are eradicated from the former ones,—that is, that three of the principal leaders are killed by Antichrist: that the other seven give him honor and wisdom and power, of whom he says:—

16. "These shall hate the whore, to wit, the city, and shall burn her flesh with fire."] Now that one of the heads was, as it were, slain to death, and that the stroke of his death was directed, he speaks of Nero. For it is plain that when the cavalry sent by the senate was pursuing him, he himself cut his throat. Him therefore, when raised up, God will send as a worthy king, but worthy in such a way as the Jews merited. And since he is to have another name, He shall also appoint another name, that so the Jews may receive him as if he were the Christ. Says Daniel: "He shall not know the lust of women, although before he was most impure, and he shall know no God of his fathers: for he will not be able to seduce the people of the circumcision, unless he is a judge of the law." Finally, also, he will recall the saints, not to the worship of idols, but to undertake circumcision, and, if he is able, to seduce any; for he shall so conduct himself as to be called Christ by them. But that he rises again from hell, we have said

above in the word of Isaiah: "Water shall nourish him, and hell hath increased him;" who, however, must come with name unchanged, and doings unchanged, as says the Spirit.

From the nineteenth chapter.

11. "And I saw heaven opened, and behold a white horse; and he that sat upon him was called Faithful and True."] The horse, and He that sits upon him, sets forth our Lord coming to His kingdom with the heavenly army. Because from the sea of the north, which is the Arabian Sea, even to the sea of Phoenice, and even to the ends of the earth, they will command these greater parts in the coming of the Lord Jesus, and all the souls of the nations will be assembled to judgment.

From the twentieth chapter.

1–3. "And I saw an angel come down from heaven, having the key of the abyss, and a chain in his hand. And he held the dragon, that old serpent, which is called the Devil and Satan, and bound him for a thousand years, and cast him into the abyss, and shut him up, and set a seal upon him, that he should deceive the nations no more, till the thousand years should be finished: after this he must be loosed a little season."] Those years wherein Satan is bound are in the first advent of Christ, even to the end of the age; and they are called a thousand, according to that mode of speaking, wherein a part is signified by the whole, just as is that passage, "the word which He commanded for a thousand generations," although they are not a thousand. Moreover that he says, "and he cast him into the abyss," he says this, because the devil, excluded from the hearts of believers, began to take possession of the wicked, in whose hearts, blinded day by day, he is shut up as if in a profound abyss. And he shut him up, says he, and put a seal upon him, that he should not deceive the nations until the thousand years should be finished. "He shut the door upon him," it is said, that is, he forbade and restrained his seducing those who belong to Christ. Moreover, he put a seal upon him, because it is hidden who belong to the side of the devil, and who to that of Christ. For we know not of those who seem to stand whether they shall not fall, and of those who are down it is uncertain whether they may rise. Moreover, that he says that he is bound and shut up, that he may not seduce the nations, the nations signify the Church, seeing that of them it itself is formed, and which being seduced, he previously held until, he says, the thousand years should be completed, that is, what is left of the sixth day, to wit, of the sixth age, which subsists for a thousand years; after this he must be loosed for a little season. The little season signifies three years and six months, in which with all his power the devil will avenge himself under Antichrist against the Church. Finally, he says, after that the devil shall be loosed, and will seduce the nations in the whole world, and will entice war against the Church, the number of whose foes shall be as the sand of the sea.

4, 5. "And I saw thrones, and them that sat upon them, and judgment was given unto them; and *I saw* the souls of them that were slain on account of the testimony of Jesus, and for the word of God, and which had not worshipped the beast nor his image, nor have received his writing on their forehead or in their hand; and they reigned with Christ for a thousand years: the rest of them lived not again until the thousand years were finished. This is the first resurrection."] There are two resurrections. But the first resurrection is now of the souls that are by the faith, which does not permit men to pass over to the second death. Of this resurrection the apostle says: "If ye have risen with Christ, seek those things which are above."

6. "Blessed and holy is he who has part in this resurrection: on them the second death shall have no power, but they shall be priests of God and Christ, and they shall reign with Him a thousand years."] I do not think the reign of a thousand years is eternal; or if it is thus to be thought of, they cease to reign when the thousand years are finished. But I will put forward what my capacity enables me to judge. The tenfold number signifies the decalogue, and the hundredfold sets forth the crown of virginity: for he who shall have kept the undertaking of virginity completely, and shall have faithfully fulfilled the precepts of the decalogue, and shall have destroyed the untrained nature or impure thoughts within the retirement of the heart, that they may not rule over him, this is the true priest of Christ, and accomplishing the millenary number thoroughly, is thought to reign with Christ; and truly in his case the devil is bound. But he who is entangled in the vices and the dogmas of heretics, in his case the devil is loosed. But that it says that when the thousand years are finished he is loosed, so the number of the perfect saints being completed, in whom there is the glory of virginity in body and mind, by the approaching advent of the kingdom of the hateful one, many, seduced by that love of earthly things, shall be overthrown, and together with him shall enter the lake of fire.

8–10. "And they went up upon the breadth of the earth, and compassed the camp of the saints about, and the beloved city; and fire came down from God out of heaven, and devoured them. And the devil who seduced them was cast into the lake of fire and brimstone, where both the beast and the false prophet shall be tormented day and night for ever and ever."] This belongs to the last judgment. And after a little time the earth was made holy, as being at least that wherein lately had reposed the bodies of the virgins, when they shall enter upon an eternal kingdom with an immortal King, as they who are not only virgins in body, but, moreover, with equal inviolability have protected themselves, both in tongue and thought, from wickedness; and these, it shows, shall dwell in rejoicing forever with the Lamb.

From the twenty-first and twenty-second chapters.

16. "And the city is placed in a square."] The city which he says is squared, he says also is resplendent with gold and precious stones, and has a sacred street, and a river through the midst of it, and the tree of life on either side, bearing twelve manner of fruits throughout the twelve months; and that the light of the sun is not there, because the Lamb is the light of it; and that its gates were of single pearls; and that there were three gates on each of the four sides, and that they could not be shut. I say, in respect of the square city, he shows forth the united multitude of the saints, in whom the faith could by no means waver. As Noah is commanded to make the ark of squared beams, that it might resist the force of the deluge, by the precious stones he sets forth the holy men who

cannot waver in persecution, who could not be moved either by the tempest of persecutors, or be dissolved from the true faith by the force of the rain, because they are associated of pure gold, of whom the city of the great King is adorned. Moreover, the streets set forth their hearts purified from all uncleanness, transparent with glowing light, that the Lord may justly walk up and down in them. The river of life sets forth that the grace of spiritual doctrine flowed through the minds of the faithful, and that manifold flourishing forms of odors germinated therein. The tree of life on either bank sets forth the Advent of Christ, according to the flesh, who satisfied the peoples wasted with famine, *that* received life from One by the wood of the Cross, with the announcement of God's word. And *in* that he says that the sun is not necessary in the city, *he* shows, evidently, that the Creator as the immaculate light shines in the midst of it, whose brightness no mind has been able to conceive, nor tongue to tell.

In that he says there are three gates placed on each of the four sides, of single pearls, I think that these are the four virtues, to wit, prudence, fortitude, justice, temperance, which are associated with one another. And, being involved together, they make the number twelve. But the twelve gates we believe to be the number of the apostles, who, shining in the four virtues as precious stones, manifesting the light of their doctrine among the saints, cause it to enter the celestial city, that by intercourse with them the choir of angels may be gladdened. And that the gates cannot be shut, it is evidently shown that the doctrine of the apostles can be separated from rectitude by no tempest of contradiction. Even though the floods of the nations and the vain superstitions of heretics should revolt against their true faith, they are overcome, and shall be dissolved as the foam, because Christ is the Rock by which, and on which, the Church is founded. And thus it is overcome by no traces of maddened men. Therefore they are not to be heard who assure themselves that there is to be an earthly reign of a thousand years; who think, *that is to say*, with the heretic Cerinthus. For the kingdom of Christ is now eternal in the saints, although the glory of the saints shall be manifested after the resurrection.

GENERAL NOTES BY THE AMERICAN EDITOR

1. The whole subject of the Apocalypse is so treated, in the *Speaker's Commentary*, as to elucidate many questions suggested by the primitive commentators of this series, and to furnish the latest judgments of critics on the subject. It is so immense a matter, however, as to render annotations on patristic *specialties* impossible in a work like this. Every reader must feel how apposite is the sententious saying of Augustine: "Apocalypsis Joannis tot sacramenta quot verba."

2. *The seven spirits*, p. 344, ver. 4. That is, the one Spirit in His seven-fold gifts. He now fulfills the promise of Christ, "He shall show you things to come." Without this complement the Church would lack assurance that her great Head upon the throne has ordered and limited the whole course of this world for her conflicts and her final triumph by the Spirit's power. St. John's rapture was the Spirit's work: "I was in the Spirit on the Lord's day." The whole Apocalypse is an Easter sermon (on the text, i. 18) and an Easter song (vers. 9-14, and *passim*). It

supplements the appearances of the risen Redeemer for *identification*, by a manifestation, which is the Church's assurance of His *glorification*, and of His perpetual work in her and for her, as well as of His presence with her, by the Spirit.

3. *Seven golden candlesticks*, p. 344, ver. 12. The symbol of the seven-fold Spirit in the Church. On the Arch of Titus this symbol had just been set up as proof of its removal from the Mosaic Church. It is now found to be transferred to the "seven churches," a symbol of the Catholic Church or the "communion of saints." The threatening of removal from particular churches derives force from the (then) recent removal out of Jerusalem.

4. *All the Saints shall assemble*, p. 345, ver. 15. Our author clings to the purer Chiliasm of Commodian, to which Augustine had now given the death-blow by his famous retraction.

5. *New forms of prophesying,* p. 347, ver.17. A retrospective glance at Montanism, and a *caveat* against the mistakes of Tertullian.

6. *I will vomit thee,* p. 347, ver. 17. Bishop Wordsworth suggests, that, if the canon of Scripture compiled by the church of Laodicea lacks the Apocalypse, its terrible reproof of that church may have influenced its unwillingness to accept it. Accordingly she was *vomited*, and perished in the Saracen invasion.

7. *That is the Spirit,* p. 348, ver. 1. Christ's divine nature as distinguished from his flesh.

"In a word," says Professor Milligan, "πνευμα is a short expression for our Lord's resurrection state." A truth, but based on the distinction between the flesh of Christ and His spiritual nature as the Word. See

Tertullian, vol. iii. p. 609, note 5, and p. 610, note 5: also 2 Cor. iii. 17-18.

8. *The genealogy of Mary,* p. 348, vers. 7-10. It is remarkable that St. Matthew should be credited with this, and not St. Luke, who in the sixteenth century began to be regarded as giving the ancestry of Mary. See Africanus on the subject, and my elucidation, in which I followed Wordsworth. Though I had already prepared the pages of Victorinus for the press, I failed to note at that time this modification of the general truth, that antiquity regards both genealogies as those of Joseph.

9. *Dan himself,* p. 349, ver. 8. Here is a touch of Chiliasm again, i.e., of the better sort. Even Dan is promised a restoration: and the use of Gen. xlix. 16 for that intent is noteworthy, as compared with Rev. vii. 5-8, where Dan is omitted. But Hippolytus takes a very different view of the same text.229

10. *Hades,* p. 351. "A region withdrawn from punishment and fires," says our author. He identifies it with paradise, and shows that in his day the Latin churches knew of no purgatorial fires. He knows of nothing but a place for those "who die in the Lord," and a place for the wicked. It is perpetually overlooked, that, in the fiction of "purgatory," it is only the righteous who are entitled to it: none but those dying in full communion with the Church having any portion in it, or any title to Masses for their repose. Of all this our author had no conception.230

11. *To take the book and eat it up,* p. 353, ver. 10. We must not fail to note with this the passage Jer. xv. 16, where the Revised Version pedantically sacrifices the Septuagint reading, ὁ λόγος σου, (which is followed by the Vulgate), distinguishing "sermones tui" from

"Verbum tuum." The Seventy have testified to this distinction in their day, and their copies of the Hebrew must have supported it. So understood, what riches in the text of Jeremiah!

12. *Thessalonians,* p. 354, ver. 7. On which much that is suggestive is said by St. Augustine, though he confesses, concerning what St. Paul had said to the Thessalonians, "Ego prorsus quid dixerit me fateor ignorare." See *De Civ. Dei,* lib. xx. cap. 19, p. 685, ed. Migne.

13. *The woman,* p. 355, ver. 1. Compare vol. vi. p. 337, note 4, and Elucidation II. p. 355. It is quite important to observe the voice of antiquity on a matter which, in our own times, has been made a stumbling-block to souls by a wanton, personal act of the Bishop of Rome and his dogma of the "Immaculate Conception."

14. *The hope of those that sleep,* p. 355, ver. 1. To make our author consistent with himself (see note 10, *supra*), we should read thus: "But they have in their darkness a light (some think) such as the moon." Here, however, it seems to me, he is giving his mind to "the Church of Fathers and Prophets" exclusively, in which *its* "saints and apostles" were for a time waiting and looking for the Man-child. Even that Church of the Hebrews had, in Hades, light "like that of the moon," where they reposed in Abraham's bosom; but Christ removed them into a fairer region, i.e., Paradise, when He illuminated Hades, and then became "the first-fruits of them that slept." Such seems to be the sense.

15. *In a certain Greek codex,* p. 357, ver. 18. Can αντεμος here be a reference to Anthemius, of the kindred of Julian (*d.* a.d. 472)? His history, mixed up with that of Ricimer, connects with Genseric, who died a.d. 477.

16. *Sea of the north,* p. 358, ver. 11. The Mediterranean, near Mount Carmel, is "the sea of Phoenice," I suppose: but how the Arabian Gulf can be called the sea of the north, I do not comprehend. As Routh says, the manuscripts must have been much corrupted.

17. *Two resurrections,* p. 359, ver. 5. Here our author, who is supposed to be the contemporary of St. Augustine, accepts his final judgment. But Victorinus was a Chiliast of the better sort, according to St. Jerome. This confirms the corruption of the mss. Indeed, if the Victorinus mentioned by Jerome be the same as our author, the mention of Genseric proves the subsequent interpolation of his works.

18. It is evident that the fragment which is here preserved, if, indeed, it be the work of Caius Marius Victorinus, surnamed Afer, is full of the corrections of some pious disciple of St. Augustine who lived much later. The reader must consult Lardner, and compare Routh, whose notes on this treatise are indeed few. He does not think the reference to *abbots* of any consequence in determining its age, because he finds albatorum elsewhere sustained as the true reading, i.e., those "*made white* in the blood of the Lamb." But the great probability that there were two authors of the name living in different ages seems more than suspected by the learned. Dupin, who calls him *Marius* without the *Caius* (changed to *Fabius* by the English translator), leaves one yet more in a mist as to the identity of our author with the one he writes about.

Victorinus

Find this and other great works of the Early Church Fathers at lighthousechristianpublishing.com.

Our Father who art in heaven, hallowed be thy name.
Thy kingdom come, Thy will be done, on earth as it is in heaven.
Give us this day our daily bread and forgive us our trespasses as we forgive those who trespass against us.
And lead us not into temptation, but deliver us from evil, for Thine is the kingdom, the power and the glory. Forever and ever.

Amen

Hail Mary full of grace, the Lord is with thee. Blessed art thou amongst women and blessed is the fruit of thy womb Jesus. Holy Mary mother of God, pray for us sinners, now and the hour of our death.

www.ingramcontent.com/pod-product-compliance
Lightning Source LLC
Chambersburg PA
CBHW050226100526
44585CB00017BA/2084